Down Under: A History

Josh Jones

Copyright Notice

Copyright © 2024 by Josh Jones. All rights reserved. No part of this publication may be reproduced, distributed, or transmitted in any form or by any means, including photocopying, recording, or other electronic or mechanical methods, without the prior written permission of the publisher, except in the case of brief quotations embodied in critical reviews and certain other noncommercial uses permitted by copyright law.

Disclaimer

This book is a work of historical interpretation and should be read as such. While the author has made every effort to ensure the accuracy of the information herein, the book is provided "as is," and the publisher and author disclaim any and all warranties, express or implied, regarding the completeness, accuracy, reliability, suitability, or availability with respect to the contents of the book.

To the spirit of Australia - its land, its people, and its enduring legacy. May we always remember where we've come from as we journey to where we're going.

In a land where histories weave, Under Southern stars, we believe, From Dreamtime to cities that gleam, A story of contrasts, a collective dream. Ancient voices echo in the red desert's heart, Modern dreams in urban art, From gold rushes to battles fought, A tapestry of lessons taught. "Down Under," where tales entwine, Of courage, struggle, and a sun that shines, Josh Jones, through pages, does reveal, A history, a journey, a land so real.

Forward

As we stand on the precipice of a new era, it is with profound reflection that we delve into the pages of this historical compendium, a testament to the enduring spirit and resilience of Australia. The journey through Australia's past is not merely an academic pursuit but a voyage of discovery, understanding, and, most importantly, recognition of the diverse narratives that have shaped this nation.

In embarking on this exploration, we are reminded of the complexity and richness of Australia's history, from the ancient wisdom of its Indigenous peoples to the ambitious visions that fuelled its modern achievements. Each chapter within this book serves as a beacon, illuminating the trials, triumphs, and transformations that have defined Australia's identity.

As your guide through these pages, I invite you to approach each story with an open heart and a curious mind. The events chronicled here are not just historical facts; they are the lived experiences of individuals and communities, each contributing a unique thread to the fabric of the nation. Through understanding these stories, we gain insight into the forces that have driven change and the values that continue to underpin Australian society.

This historical journey is also a mirror, reflecting the broader challenges and aspirations of humanity. Australia's story is one of adaptation and resilience, of confronting adversity with courage and forging unity from diversity. It is a narrative that resonates beyond its geographical confines, offering lessons and inspiration for all who seek to navigate the complexities of our shared global history.

As we turn these pages, let us also look forward, envisioning the future chapters yet to be written in Australia's history. The past, with all its intricacies and contradictions, provides us with the wisdom to move forward, to build a more inclusive, equitable, and sustainable world.

In closing, I extend my gratitude to you, the reader, for embarking on this journey. May the stories within these pages ignite a passion for discovery and a deeper appreciation for the rich tapestry of human experience that is Australia's history.

With warm regards,

Rose Hylos

In 1770, a pivotal moment in the annals of exploration and colonial expansion was etched into the fabric of history as Captain James Cook, commanding the HMS Endeavour, navigated the uncharted waters of Australia's east coast. This journey not only marked a significant geographical discovery but also heralded the beginning of a new era in the relationship between the indigenous peoples of the continent and European settlers.

The Endeavour, a British Royal Navy research vessel, set sail from Plymouth in 1768 with the dual mission of observing the transit of Venus across the sun in Tahiti and to seek the mysterious Terra Australis Incognita, a land believed to exist in the southern hemisphere. Cook, an experienced and skilled navigator, led his crew on this ambitious voyage that would eventually change the course of Australian history.

As the Endeavour made its way through the Pacific, Cook and his crew encountered myriad challenges, from treacherous seas to the threat of scurvy, a common affliction among sailors due to a lack of fresh food. Nevertheless, Cook's leadership and the crew's resilience saw them through these trials, showcasing the determination and fortitude that characterised this era of exploration.

Upon sighting the eastern coastline of Australia in April 1770, Cook and his crew became the first Europeans to document this vast and diverse landscape. The Endeavour made landfall at a place Cook named Botany Bay, so-called because of the abundance of unique plants discovered by the ship's botanists, Joseph Banks and Daniel Solander. This encounter was not merely a scientific expedition; it was the first meeting of two vastly different cultures. The indigenous people observed the strange new arrivals with curiosity and caution, an interaction that marked the beginning of a complex and often troubled relationship.

Cook's voyage along the coast was meticulous. He charted the coastline with remarkable accuracy, naming landmarks and taking note of potential harbours. The Great Barrier Reef proved a formidable obstacle, nearly claiming the Endeavour as it ran aground on the coral. The crew's desperate efforts to repair the ship highlighted their vulnerability in this remote part of the world and underscored the dangers of exploration. After weeks of repairs on the banks of the Endeavour River, the voyage continued, further mapping the coastline and asserting British interest in this new land.

The significance of Cook's journey cannot be overstated. It opened the eastern coast of Australia to European eyes, providing detailed charts and a wealth of scientific knowledge that would pave the way for future colonisation. Cook's claim of the east coast for Britain under the doctrine of terra nullius—ignoring the existence of the indigenous populations—set in motion events that would lead to the establishment of a penal colony in New South Wales in 1788.

This chapter of exploration is marked by contrasts: the excitement of discovery against the backdrop of impending colonisation and the inevitable clash of cultures it would entail. Cook's voyage is celebrated for its contributions to navigation, science, and geography, yet it also foreshadows the trials and tribulations that would befall the continent's original inhabitants and the environmental impacts that exploration and settlement would have on the land.

In recounting the journey of the Endeavour, we are reminded of the courage and curiosity that drive human exploration. Captain James Cook's voyage along the east coast of Australia is a seminal event that not only expanded the boundaries of the known world but also set the stage for the complex tapestry of Australian history that would unfold in the centuries to come.

In the annals of Australian history, the year 1788 stands as a watershed moment, marking the establishment of the first British colony on the continent's shores. The arrival of the First Fleet at Port Jackson, under the command of Captain Arthur Phillip, signified the beginning of European settlement and the imposition of British sovereignty over the eastern part of Australia, an act that would have profound and lasting effects on the continent's indigenous peoples and its ecological landscape.

The decision to establish a penal colony in New South Wales was driven by several factors. The loss of the American colonies had deprived Britain of a vital outlet for the relocation of convicts, an issue compounded by overcrowded prisons and prison ships, known as hulks, moored along the

Thames. Additionally, strategic considerations, including the desire to pre-empt French colonial ambitions in the Pacific, played a crucial role in the British government's decision to colonise New South Wales.

On 13 May 1787, the First Fleet, comprising eleven ships and carrying over 1,000 passengers, including marines, seamen, civil officers, and convicts, set sail from Portsmouth, England. The fleet, a microcosm of British society's lower rungs, undertook a perilous eight-month voyage, navigating the world's vast and uncertain oceans to reach the Australian continent.

Upon arrival at Botany Bay in January 1788, Captain Phillip quickly realised that the bay was unsuitable for settlement due to poor soil and a lack of fresh water. Consequently, he explored further north, discovering the more favourable Port Jackson, a harbour with deep anchorage and fresh water. On 26 January, now commemorated as Australia Day, the British flag was hoisted at Sydney Cove, signifying the official establishment of the colony of New South Wales.

The early years of the colony were fraught with hardships. The settlers faced challenges in adapting to the unfamiliar environment, with food shortages common and initial attempts at agriculture largely unsuccessful. The convicts, many of whom were urban poor from Britain, lacked the skills necessary for survival in what was perceived as a harsh and inhospitable land. Relations with the indigenous peoples, who had inhabited the continent for over 65,000 years, were complex and often marked by conflict, as the arrival of the settlers disrupted their traditional way of life, leading to dispossession, disease, and violence.

Governor Phillip, aware of the difficulties, sought to establish a viable community, enacting measures to maintain discipline and order while also exploring the potential for economic development. His policies towards the Indigenous Australians were initially conciliatory; however, cultural misunderstandings and competition for resources strained these relations.

The significance of 1788 extends beyond the mere establishment of a penal colony; it represents the beginning of a dramatic transformation of the Australian continent. The introduction of European farming practices, animals, and plants, along with the subsequent waves of migration, altered the landscape and initiated a series of changes that would have enduring impacts on Australia's ecological systems and its indigenous cultures.

This chapter in Australia's history encapsulates a period of profound change, characterised by the collision of worlds. The establishment of the first British colony in New South Wales laid the foundations for the development of modern Australia, setting the stage for its evolution from a penal colony to a prosperous nation. Yet, it also marks the commencement of a darker period for the continent's indigenous peoples, whose cultures and livelihoods were irrevocably altered by European colonisation. The legacy of 1788 is thus a complex tapestry, woven from threads of discovery, hardship, and the indomitable human spirit, but also of dispossession and conflict, themes that c

In the year 1803, the British Empire, eager to expand its colonial reach and assert its dominance in the Southern Hemisphere, took a decisive step by establishing the first European settlement on the island that would later be known as Tasmania. This move was not merely an extension of Britain's colonial ambitions but a strategic manoeuvre aimed at deterring French interests in the region, amid the global tensions of the Napoleonic Wars. The island, then known by its indigenous name Van Diemen's Land, named after Anthony van Diemen, the Governor-General of the Dutch East Indies who had commissioned Abel Tasman's voyage of discovery in 1642, was to become a new frontier for the British penal colony system.

Lieutenant John Bowen, a young

officer of the Royal Navy, was tasked with the mission of establishing this outpost. Bowen, commanding a small contingent of soldiers, free settlers, and convicts, arrived at Risdon Cove on the eastern bank of the Derwent River in September 1803. This site was chosen for its strategic advantages, including access to fresh water and the potential for defensive fortifications, crucial considerations given the perceived threat of French naval activity in the region.

The early days of the settlement were marked by immense hardship and adversity. The settlers struggled with the unfamiliar environment, experiencing shortages of food and supplies, which were exacerbated by the logistical challenges of maintaining a supply line over such vast distances from the main colony in New South

Wales and the British Isles. Moreover, the initial interactions between the European settlers and the indigenous Tasmanian communities, who had inhabited the island for over 40,000 years, were fraught with misunderstandings and conflicts. These tensions were rooted in the profound disruption that the establishment of the settlement posed to the indigenous way of life, including competition for resources and the Europeans' encroachment on their lands.

Despite these challenges, the settlement at Risdon Cove was the beginning of a permanent European presence in Tasmania. In the years that followed, the colony would grow, both in size and in its economic importance to the British Empire. The discovery of fertile lands and the expansion of agricultural activities, particularly sheep farming, played a significant role in this development. However, this expansion came at a significant cost to the island's indigenous population, leading to the tragic conflicts known as the Black War, which would decimate the indigenous Tasmanians in the ensuing decades.

The establishment of the first settlement in Tasmania in 1803 is a chapter of contrast and conflict in Australian history. It represents the extension of European exploration and colonisation, driven by strategic imperatives and the pursuit of economic opportunities. Yet, it also marks the beginning of a period of profound suffering and dispossession for the indigenous population of Tasmania. The legacy of this chapter is complex, encapsulating themes of exploration, settlement, and conflict that are central to understanding the broader narrative of Australia's colonial past.

As the settlement grew and evolved, it became a pivotal point for further exploration and settlement within Tasmania and a critical component of the British penal colony network. The establishment of Hobart, following the relocation of the main settlement from Risdon Cove to Sullivan's Cove in 1804 by Lieutenant-Governor David Collins, signalled the burgeoning importance of Tasmania within the colonial enterprise. This development laid the groundwork for the transformation of the island into a key agricultural and penal colony within the British Empire.

The story of 1803 and the establishment of the first settlement in Tasmania is thus a foundational episode in the history of Australia. It reflects the broader themes of European colonial expansion, the clash of cultures, and the environmental and human consequences of colonisation. As such, it provides essential insights into the complex and often contentious history of Australia's development as a nation.

In 1829, the British Empire, driven by its insatiable appetite for expansion and strategic positioning, undertook the establishment of the Swan River Colony on the western coast of Australia. This event marked the beginning of European settlement in an area that would later evolve into the vibrant city of Perth and its surrounding regions. Unlike the penal colonies of the eastern seaboard, the Swan River Colony was envisioned as a free settlement, attracting settlers with the promise of land grants and the opportunity to forge a new life in a distant land.

The origins of the Swan River Colony can be traced back to exploratory voyages and the British government's growing concern over French naval exploration in the Indian Ocean and the western coast of Australia. Captain

James Stirling, aboard the HMS Success, conducted a detailed exploration of the region in 1827. Stirling's reports, which painted a picture of fertile lands and a favourable climate, were instrumental in convincing the British authorities of the viability of a new settlement.

The official proclamation of the Swan River Colony in June 1829 marked a significant expansion of British influence on the Australian continent. The settlement was named after the prominent river winding through the land, identified by Dutch explorers in the 17th century and later named by the British. The area around the Swan River was deemed suitable for agriculture, which was a crucial factor in the decision to establish the colony.

The early settlers of the Swan River

Colony, a mix of British and Irish emigrants, faced immense challenges. The land, while promising in Captain Stirling's reports, proved difficult to cultivate. The sandy soil, lack of fresh water, and the settlers' general inexperience with the harsh Australian environment led to initial failures in establishing successful farms. Moreover, the expectations of a bountiful new Eden were quickly tempered by the reality of the hard work required to tame the land.

In addition to agricultural challenges, the settlers' presence disrupted the lives of the indigenous Noongar people, leading to tensions and conflicts. The Noongar people, who had lived in the southwestern part of Australia for thousands of years, found their traditional hunting grounds and water sources threatened by the encroachment of European settlers. The resulting clashes were part of the broader pattern of dispossession and violence that marked the colonial expansion across Australia.

Despite these early difficulties, the Swan River Colony gradually began to prosper. The discovery of fertile tracts of land in the surrounding areas, improvements in agricultural techniques, and the establishment of trade links with other colonies contributed to the colony's growth. Perth, named after the Scottish birthplace of Sir George Murray, then British Secretary of State for the Colonies, emerged as the administrative and commercial centre of the colony.

The establishment of the Swan River Colony in 1829 is a chapter of both vision and hardship. It reflects the broader themes of British colonial ambition, the lure of new beginnings, and the complex interactions between European settlers and indigenous populations. The colony's transformation from a struggling settlement into the thriving city of Perth and its surrounding communities is a testament to the determination and resilience of its early inhabitants.

This period in Western Australia's history is pivotal for understanding the state's development and the broader narrative of Australian colonisation. The Swan River Colony laid the foundations for Western Australia's unique character within the federation, characterised by a distinct history of settlement and development. As such, the establishment of the colony in 1829 remains a significant milestone in the tapestry of Australia's colonial past, marking the beginning of a new chapter in the continent's complex and multifaceted history.

In 1851, the discovery of gold in New South Wales and Victoria marked a turning point in Australian history, catalysing a series of gold rushes that would transform the social, economic, and political landscape of the continent. These discoveries attracted people from all over the world, drawn by the allure of wealth and the promise of a new life, thereby accelerating the population growth and development of Australia's colonies.

The first officially recognised discovery of gold occurred near Bathurst, New South Wales, in February 1851, when Edward Hargraves, who had returned from the Californian goldfields, identified a payable goldfield. Hargraves, aided by John Lister and brothers William and James Tom, found five specks of alluvial gold at Ophir. This discovery was pivotal, not merely for its immediate impact but for how it symbolised the untapped wealth of the Australian continent. Following this revelation, Governor FitzRoy authorised the issuance of licences to prospect for gold, effectively opening the floodgates to would-be fortune seekers.

Victoria's gold rush began shortly after, with the first significant finds near Clunes in July 1851, followed by richer discoveries at Ballarat and Bendigo. These finds were of unprecedented scale, with the Ballarat and Bendigo fields becoming some of the world's richest, drawing a global influx of miners. The Victorian goldfields, with their vast wealth, became the epicentre of a gold rush that would see the colony's population swell from 77,000 in 1851 to 540,000 by 1861.

The gold rushes brought profound change. Towns sprang up around the diggings, some, like those at Ballarat and Bendigo, enduring and growing into major cities, while others, once the gold dwindled, faded into ghost towns. The demographic shift was equally significant; the goldfields attracted a diverse international population, including significant numbers from China, contributing to the multicultural character of modern Australia.

Economically, the gold rushes were transformative. The wealth generated financed infrastructure development, including roads, railways, and telegraphs, linking isolated communities and facilitating commerce and communication. Additionally, the influx of wealth and people boosted demand for goods and services, stimulating local industries and agriculture.

Socially, the goldfields were places of both opportunity and exploitation. The promise of wealth was real for some, with spectacular finds creating fortunes overnight. However, for many, the reality was harsh, with backbreaking labour, lawlessness, and competition for claims. The significant Chinese population on the goldfields faced particular discrimination, leading to tensions and riots, such as those at Lambing Flat in New South Wales.

Politically, the gold rushes had a lasting impact on Australian society. The influx of wealth and population challenged the colonial authorities and laid the groundwork for democratic reforms. The Eureka Stockade uprising in 1854, sparked by miner opposition to licence fees and perceived injustices, is often cited as a seminal moment in the development of Australian democracy.

The discovery of gold in New South Wales and Victoria in 1851 thus stands as a cornerstone event in Australian history. It accelerated the transition from a collection of British penal colonies to a dynamic set of communities marked by rapid population growth, economic development, and social change. The legacies of the gold rushes are manifold, influencing the nation's character, its demographic composition, and its path towards federation in 1901. This chapter in Australia's story reflects the transformative power of gold, not just in wealth but in the dreams it inspired and the realities it forged on the distant shores of a continent undergoing profound change.

In 1856, Victoria became a pioneering force in the evolution of democratic processes by introducing the secret ballot for electoral voting, a revolutionary development that significantly influenced democratic practices worldwide. Prior to this reform, voting was conducted publicly, either by a show of hands or by verbal declaration, a method that was susceptible to undue influence, intimidation, and corruption. The introduction of the secret ballot, therefore, marked a significant leap forward in the pursuit of free and fair elections, ensuring that voters could cast their votes without fear of repercussion.

The push for the secret ballot emerged from growing concerns over electoral corruption and the manipulation of voters by landlords, employers, and other powerful figures. The gold rushes of the 1850s had brought a dramatic increase in the population and wealth of Victoria, alongside a more vibrant and diverse society. This period of rapid change fuelled demands for political reform and greater representation, leading to the granting of responsible government to Victoria in 1855.

The Victorian Electoral Act of 1856 was the legislative response to these demands, enacting the secret ballot, which came to be known colloquially as the "Australian ballot." The Act required that voting be conducted using printed ballots listing the names of candidates, which were marked in the privacy of a voting booth. This process was designed to protect the voter's choice from being disclosed, thereby eliminating the potential for coercion.

The introduction of the secret ballot in Victoria was met with considerable interest and admiration from other colonies and countries, many of which were grappling with similar issues of electoral reform. The success of the system in Victoria led to its adoption in other Australian colonies and its eventual spread to other parts of the British Empire and beyond. The "Australian ballot" became a model for electoral reform, influencing countries across the world to adopt similar measures to safeguard the integrity of their electoral processes.

The implementation of the secret ballot had immediate and far-reaching effects on Victorian society and politics. It levelled the electoral playing field, giving a voice to the previously disenfranchised and reducing the power of the elite to dictate electoral outcomes. This reform contributed to the development of a more egalitarian society, in which the principles of democracy were more fully realised.

Moreover, the secret ballot facilitated greater political participation and engagement, as voters were more likely to exercise their right to vote when assured of the confidentiality of their choices. This increase in participation was crucial in a period marked by significant social and economic transformation, ensuring that the evolving needs and opinions of the populace were more accurately reflected in the political process.

The introduction of the secret ballot in Victoria in 1856 stands as a landmark event in the history of democracy. It not only transformed electoral practices within the colony but also set a precedent that would have a lasting impact on the democratic world. By ensuring the privacy and integrity of the voting process, Victoria contributed to the strengthening of democratic institutions and the promotion of political rights and freedoms. This achievement is a testament to the colony's progressive spirit and its commitment to the principles of justice and equality, serving as a crucial chapter in the broader narrative of democratic evolution.

The Burke and Wills expedition of 1860-1861 stands as one of the most ambitious and tragic episodes in the exploration of the Australian continent. Undertaken with the intention of crossing Australia from south to north, from Melbourne in Victoria to the Gulf of Carpentaria in Queensland, this expedition aimed to fill the vast blanks on the map of inland Australia and establish a route across the continent. The journey not only tested the limits of human endurance and resolve but also laid bare the harsh and unforgiving nature of Australia's interior.

Led by Robert O'Hara Burke, a police officer and enthusiastic explorer, and William John Wills, a surveyor and scientist, the expedition was equipped with the latest technology and supplies. It comprised a large team of men, along with camels and horses, intended to sustain them over the expected six-month journey. The Victorian government, keen on the potential economic benefits of such an exploration and the prestige of achieving a continental crossing, heavily funded the expedition.

Departing Melbourne in August 1860 amid public fanfare, the expedition made its way northward, facing immediate challenges. The cumbersome size of the party, the inexperience of its members in bushcraft and navigation, and the logistical difficulties of transporting their extensive supplies slowed their progress considerably. As they advanced, the terrain became increasingly arid and difficult to traverse, presenting significant obstacles to their advance.

By December 1860, Burke, impatient with the slow pace, decided to push forward with a smaller party, including Wills, John King, and Charles Gray, leaving the rest of the team at a base camp at Cooper's Creek. This decision would have dire consequences. The smaller party reached the northern coast near the Gulf of Carpentaria by February 1861 but was unable to reach the open sea due to the mangrove swamps blocking their path. Exhausted and with supplies dwindling, they commenced the return journey to Cooper's Creek.

Upon their return to the base camp in April 1861, they found it deserted, the rest of the team having waited as long as they could before leaving for Melbourne, believing Burke and his party to have perished. A tree at the campsite bore the carving "DIG", indicating that provisions had been buried there for their use. Despite this, weakened by hunger, exhaustion, and the onset of scurvy, the situation for Burke, Wills, King, and Gray became increasingly desperate.

In the weeks that followed, Charles Gray died, and the remaining three struggled to survive in the harsh environment. Burke and Wills eventually succumbed to their conditions, leaving John King as the sole survivor. King was found alive by a rescue party several months later, living with a local Indigenous group who had helped him survive.

The Burke and Wills expedition, despite its tragic end, had significant impacts. It demonstrated the vast and challenging nature of Australia's interior, dispelling any lingering myths of an inland sea or fertile lands awaiting development. The ordeal also highlighted the importance of Indigenous knowledge in surviving Australia's harsh environments, a fact underscored by John King's survival due to the assistance of local Aboriginal people.

The public reaction to the fate of the Burke and Wills expedition was one of shock and mourning, mixed with admiration for the explorers' bravery and determination. Memorials were erected, and the story of the expedition became a part of Australian folklore, symbolising both the dangers of underestimating Australia's interior and the spirit of exploration.

In the annals of Australian exploration, the Burke and Wills expedition remains a poignant reminder of the challenges faced by those who sought to uncover the secrets of the continent's vast interior. Their journey, marked by both ambition and tragedy, is an indelible part of the nation's history, reflecting the complex interplay between human endeavour and the formidable Australian landscape.

The year 1901 marks a seminal moment in the annals of Australian history with the Federation of the six self-governing colonies into the Commonwealth of Australia. This transformative event on the 1st of January signified the birth of a unified nation, transitioning from a collection of British colonies into a federated entity under the Crown. The journey to Federation was characterised by a series of debates, conventions, and referendums, reflecting the complexities of uniting disparate colonies with their own laws, policies, and railways into a single federation.

The call for Federation was driven by a confluence of economic, defence, and nationalistic factors. The colonies faced practical challenges in trade and communication, hindered by varying tariffs and railway gauges. Moreover, the need for a coordinated defence strategy was underscored by the growing realisation of Australia's vulnerability to external threats in a region rapidly changing under the influences of European and American imperialism. Additionally, a burgeoning sense of Australian identity, distinct from British or colonial affiliations, fostered the desire for a united nation.

The path to Federation was neither quick nor straightforward. The 1890s saw a series of constitutional conventions held, where representatives from each colony convened to draft a constitution that would underpin the new nation. The debates were intense, reflecting the diverse interests and concerns of each colony. Key issues included the distribution of powers between the federal government and the states, the structure of the Parliament, and the method of amending the constitution. The proposed constitution was a testament to compromise and negotiation, embodying the principles of federalism while ensuring the protection of states' rights.

The turning point came with the referendums held in each colony between 1898 and 1900, where the proposed constitution was put to the public. The success of these referendums, albeit after initial setbacks and revisions to the constitution, paved the way for the Commonwealth of Australia. The British Parliament subsequently passed the Commonwealth of Australia Constitution Act, and Queen Victoria assented to it on 9th July 1900, setting the stage for the formal proclamation of Federation on 1st January 1901.

The Federation of Australia was celebrated across the newly formed nation, with ceremonies and festivities marking the dawn of a new era. The first Federal Parliament was opened on 9th May 1901 by the Duke of Cornwall and York (later King George V) at the Royal Exhibition Building in Melbourne, serving as a temporary seat of government until the establishment of Canberra as the capital.

The establishment of the Commonwealth of Australia represented a remarkable achievement in voluntary colonial federation, unique in the annals of British imperialism. It created a federal system of government, with powers divided between the federal government and the states, outlined in the constitution. The Senate was established to represent the states, while the House of Representatives represented the population, ensuring both regional and democratic representation.

Federation also set the foundation for the development of a distinct national identity, fostering a sense of unity and common purpose among Australians. It facilitated the creation of national institutions and symbols, including the Australian flag and, later, the Australian Defence Force. Furthermore, it allowed for the implementation of uniform laws on immigration, trade, and defence, shaping the nation's policy directions in the years to come.

In reflecting on the Federation of Australia, it is evident that this was not merely an administrative reorganisation but a profound transformation in the idea of Australia itself. It was a vision brought to life by the collective will and aspiration of its people, seeking to build a nation that embraced both the diversity of its states and the unity of its national character. The Federation of 1901 stands as a testament to the enduring values of cooperation, negotiation, and shared identity, laying the groundwork for the Commonwealth of Australia's journey through the twentieth century and beyond.

The landing of the Australian and New Zealand Army Corps (ANZAC) at Gallipoli during the First World War on 25th April 1915 represents one of the most significant and defining moments in Australian and New Zealand history. It was a campaign conceived with the aim of securing a sea route to Russia and knocking the Ottoman Empire out of the war. However, it would come to symbolise the courage, endurance, and camaraderie of the ANZAC forces, marking the birth of a national consciousness in both countries.

The ANZAC troops were part of a larger Allied expedition that aimed to capture the Gallipoli Peninsula to open the Dardanelles to the Allied navies. The ultimate objective was to capture Constantinople (now Istanbul), the capital of the Ottoman Empire, an ally of the Central Powers. The operation was ambitious and fraught with risk, requiring a landing on the heavily fortified shores of Gallipoli.

In the early hours of 25th April, the ANZACs landed on a narrow beach, soon to be known as ANZAC Cove, on the Aegean side of the peninsula. This initial landing, intended to secure a strategic advantage and allow for the further advancement of Allied forces, was met with fierce resistance from the Ottoman defenders. The terrain, marked by steep cliffs and ridges, and the well-prepared Ottoman troops made the advance extremely difficult.

The campaign quickly became a stalemate, with neither side able to secure a decisive advantage. The ANZACs, alongside British and French troops, found themselves engaged in a protracted and brutal campaign of trench warfare, enduring harsh conditions, and suffering heavy casualties. The heat, flies, and the threat of disease added to the misery of the soldiers, as did the constant danger from sniper fire, shelling, and infantry attacks.

Despite these hardships, the ANZAC troops demonstrated remarkable resilience, bravery, and resourcefulness. The landing at Gallipoli and the subsequent fighting forged a sense of identity and camaraderie among the Australian and New Zealand troops, laying the foundations for the ANZAC legend that would become a pivotal part of the national identity of both countries. Stories of heroism, sacrifice, and mateship emerged from the campaign, epitomised by figures such as John Simpson Kirkpatrick, known as

"Simpson and his donkey," who became famous for his efforts to rescue wounded soldiers from the battlefield.

The Gallipoli campaign ultimately ended in withdrawal and defeat for the Allied forces. The decision to evacuate was made in December 1915, and by January 1916, all Allied troops had been withdrawn from the peninsula. The campaign had resulted in heavy casualties: over 8,000 Australian and nearly 3,000 New Zealand soldiers lost their lives, with many more wounded.

The impact of the Gallipoli campaign was profound, both at the time and in the years that followed. It marked the first major military action undertaken by Australian and New Zealand forces during the First World War, and its memory has been preserved through the commemoration of ANZAC Day on 25th April each year. This day has become a national day of remembrance in Australia and New Zealand, honouring not only those who served and died at Gallipoli but all who have served and died in military operations for their countries.

The legacy of Gallipoli is complex, encapsulating themes of bravery, futility, and loss. It serves as a reminder of the horrors of war and the sacrifices made by those who serve. The campaign's significance in the national consciousness of Australia and New Zealand cannot be overstated, representing a crucible in which a sense of national identity was forged through the experience of conflict and comradeship. The story of the ANZACs at Gallipoli remains an enduring chapter in the history of both nations, a testament to their spirit and resilience in the face of adversity.

The year 1923 marked a pivotal chapter in the evolution of Australia's national identity and democratic tradition with the opening of the first Parliament House in Canberra. This event was not merely an architectural or political milestone but represented the culmination of a vision for a distinct Australian nationhood, with Canberra symbolising the unity and independence of the Commonwealth of Australia. The establishment of a permanent seat for the Parliament was a testament to the country's growth and the maturing of its democratic institutions since Federation in 1901.

The decision to locate the capital in Canberra, a purpose-built city, was a result of a compromise between the two largest cities, Sydney and Melbourne, which had both vied to be the nation's capital. The site was selected in 1908, and the city's design was entrusted to the American architect Walter Burley Griffin, who envisioned Canberra as a city that harmonised with the landscape, embodying democratic ideals and aesthetic principles.

Construction of the provisional Parliament House commenced in 1923, following years of planning and debate regarding its design and location. The building was designed by John Smith Murdoch, the Chief Architect for the Commonwealth, who proposed a modest, yet dignified structure to serve as the temporary home of Australia's federal legislature until a more permanent structure could be built. This approach reflected both the pragmatic considerations of cost and the symbolic importance of establishing a legislative seat that was uniquely Australian, distinct from the colonial architectures of its past.

On 9th May 1927, the Duke of York (later King George VI) officially opened the first Parliament House, an event attended by politicians, dignitaries, and thousands of spectators from across Australia. This date was carefully chosen to coincide with the anniversary of the opening of the first Federal Parliament in Melbourne in 1901, thus linking the nation's democratic journey from its inception to its coming of age with a permanent home for its parliamentary proceedings.

The opening ceremony was imbued with a sense of national pride and optimism. It symbolised the democratic aspirations of Australia and its commitment to the principles of freedom, justice, and collective governance. The building itself, set against the backdrop of the Australian Capital Territory's rolling hills, was a modest edifice, yet it stood as a beacon of Australia's democratic values and its belief in the power of parliamentary democracy.

The first Parliament House served as the centre of Australian political life for over 60 years, witnessing debates, decisions, and legislation that shaped the nation. It was the site of significant moments in Australia's history, including the declaration of the country's involvement in World War II, the introduction of landmark legislation such as the Australia Act 1986 which severed the remaining constitutional ties to Britain, and the momentous apology to the Indigenous Stolen Generations in 2008.

The significance of the first Parliament House extends beyond its role as a legislative chamber. It embodied the ideals of a young nation striving to define its identity on the world stage. The building, and the city of Canberra itself, represented a break from Australia's colonial past, a step towards an independent future where Australians could shape their destiny.

In 1988, the Australian Parliament moved to the new and current Parliament House, built on Capital Hill, as the first had been intended as a temporary home. However, the original Parliament House, now known as Old Parliament House, remains a symbol of Australia's democratic heritage and continues to serve the public as a museum of political history.

The opening of the first Parliament

House in Canberra in 1927 was, therefore, a defining moment in Australian history. It marked the consolidation of the nation's democratic institutions and the physical manifestation of a federal unity. This chapter in Australia's story reflects not only the political aspirations of its people but also the enduring importance of democracy in shaping the Australian national identity.

The bombing of Darwin on 19th February 1942 by Japanese forces stands as one of the most significant and harrowing events in Australian history during the Second World War. This assault was the largest single attack ever mounted by a foreign power on Australia and marked a profound moment of realisation for the Australian people regarding the direct threat the war posed to their own shores. Prior to this attack, the war had seemed a distant conflict, largely fought in the deserts of North Africa, the skies over Britain, and across the vast expanses of the Pacific and Asia. The bombing of Darwin shattered this perception, bringing the stark realities of war home to the Australian continent.

On that fateful day, just before 10:00 am, a force of 188 Japanese aircraft, launched from four aircraft carriers in the Timor Sea, descended upon Darwin. The town was a key military and naval base, hosting a significant number of Allied troops and serving as a critical staging point for shipping in the Pacific Theatre. Despite intelligence reports suggesting an imminent attack, Darwin was ill-prepared for the scale and ferocity of the assault. The Japanese targeted the harbour, airfields, and town infrastructure, causing immense destruction and chaos.

The initial raid lasted approximately 40 minutes but was followed by a second wave of 54 land-based bombers later that day. The devastation was extensive: ships were sunk, buildings were demolished, and vital communication lines were cut. Official records state that 235 people were killed during the bombings, with hundreds more wounded. However, the true death toll is believed to be higher, as the records of the time were incomplete and did not account for all military and Indigenous Australian casualties.

The psychological impact of the Darwin bombings on the Australian populace was profound. The attacks dispelled any remaining illusions of the country's isolation as a safeguard against the global conflict. For the first time, the Australian mainland found itself directly in the line of fire, leading to widespread fear of an imminent Japanese invasion. This fear was compounded by subsequent air raids on northern Australia and the rapid advance of Japanese forces through Southeast Asia and the Pacific.

In response to the attack, there was a significant reorganisation of Australia's military strategy and home defence measures. Troop numbers in the northern regions were increased, and there was a concerted effort to improve air and sea defences. The bombings also reinforced the strategic importance of Australia's alliance with the United States, leading to an increased American military presence in the country and the establishment of a major base in Brisbane.

The bombing of Darwin remains a poignant reminder of the vulnerability and resilience of the Australian home front during the Second World War. It served as a catalyst for a nationwide mobilisation effort, uniting Australians in the defence of their country and in support of the broader Allied cause. The memory of the bombings has been etched into the national consciousness, commemorated annually to honour those who lost their lives and to acknowledge the enduring spirit of the survivors and the city of Darwin itself.

This chapter of Australian history, while marked by tragedy and destruction, also exemplifies the courage and solidarity exhibited by Australians in the face of adversity. It highlights the strategic shift in Australia's military engagement during the Second World War and underscores the significant impact of the Pacific conflict on Australian shores. The bombings of Darwin not only reshaped Australia's military and defensive policies but also marked a pivotal moment in the nation's wartime narrative, illustrating the direct and immediate effects of global conflict on the Australian home front.

In 1956, the city of Melbourne had the honour of hosting the Summer Olympic Games, marking a significant milestone in Australian sporting history and post-war recovery. This event was the first time the Olympics were held in the Southern Hemisphere, and in Australia, symbolising the nation's emergence onto the global stage as a country of cultural and sporting significance. The XVI Olympiad, as it was officially known, brought athletes from around the world to compete in a spirit of peace and international camaraderie, at a time when the world was still grappling with the aftermath of the Second World War and the ongoing tensions of the Cold War.

The selection of Melbourne as the host city in 1949 was met with enthusiasm and pride by Australians, who saw the Games as an opportunity to showcase their country's progress and hospitality. Preparations for the event were extensive, involving significant infrastructural developments in Melbourne, including the construction of the Melbourne Cricket Ground (MCG) as the main Olympic stadium, Olympic Park, and the Olympic Village in Heidelberg to accommodate the athletes. These developments were undertaken with a keen sense of purpose and optimism, reflecting Australia's desire to present itself as a modern, forward-looking nation.

The Games opened on 22nd November 1956, with a ceremony at the MCG attended by over 100,000 spectators, including dignitaries from around the world. The atmosphere was one of excitement and unity, as the Olympic flame, having travelled over land and sea from Olympia, was lit by

Ron Clarke, symbolising the opening of the Games. The event was notable for several reasons, not least because of the international tensions of the time, including the Suez Crisis and the Hungarian Revolution, which led to some countries boycotting or protesting during the Games.

Despite these geopolitical undercurrents, the Melbourne Olympics were characterised by moments of remarkable sporting achievement and acts of sportsmanship that captured the imagination of the world. The Games featured 3,314 athletes from 72 nations, competing in 151 events across 17 sports. One of the most memorable moments was the "Blood in the Water" water polo match between Hungary and the Soviet Union, which took place against the backdrop of the Soviet invasion of Hungary. The match was a dramatic and physical encounter, reflecting the political tensions between the two countries, and ended with victory for Hungary.

Another highlight was the performance of the Australian athletes, who enjoyed considerable success, finishing third in the medal tally behind the United States and the Soviet Union. Australian swimmers, in particular, shone brightly, with Murray Rose and Dawn Fraser becoming household names due to their outstanding achievements in the pool.

The 1956 Melbourne Olympics also left a lasting legacy in terms of sportsmanship and international friendship. The athletes' shared experiences in the Olympic Village and the mutual respect shown during competition fostered a sense of global community, encapsulated in the spontaneous act of several athletes marching together under a single banner during the closing ceremony, transcending national boundaries in a display of unity that would become a defining image of the Games.

In hosting the 1956 Summer Olympic Games, Melbourne not only provided a stage for some of the most memorable moments in Olympic history but also demonstrated Australia's capacity to unite the world through sport. The success of the Games was a testament to the organisational skills, spirit, and warmth of the Australian people, contributing significantly to the country's international reputation. The legacy of the Melbourne Olympics endures, remembered not only for the sporting achievements that took place but also for promoting peace, understanding, and goodwill among nations at a time of global uncertainty.

In 1962, a landmark legislative change unfolded within the Australian political landscape, marking a pivotal moment in the long and often fraught history of Indigenous rights in the country. This year saw the Commonwealth Electoral Act amended to finally grant all Indigenous Australians the right to vote in federal elections, a right that had been selectively applied and marred by various restrictions since the federation of Australia in 1901. This legislative change represented not merely an extension of political rights but a significant step towards the recognition of Indigenous Australians as full and equal citizens within their own country.

Prior to this amendment, the right of Indigenous Australians to vote in federal elections was a complex and often exclusionary patchwork of laws. While Indigenous men and women in some states had been able to vote in state elections if they met certain conditions, such as property ownership, their rights at the federal level were severely restricted. In Queensland and Western Australia, Indigenous Australians were explicitly barred from voting in federal elections unless they were servicemen. The 1962 amendment eradicated these inconsistencies and exclusions, affirming the principle that citizenship rights should extend to all Australians, irrespective of racial or cultural background.

The change did not emerge in a vacuum but was the culmination of a broader movement towards civil rights and recognition of Indigenous Australians, driven by both Indigenous activists and non-Indigenous allies. These groups campaigned tirelessly for equality, utilising the growing awareness and changing attitudes within both the Australian public and the international community towards racial discrimination. Their efforts were part of a larger global civil rights movement that sought to challenge and dismantle institutionalised racism and colonial legacies.

The decision to extend voting rights to all Indigenous Australians was made by the Liberal-Country Party government led by Prime Minister Robert Menzies. It reflected an evolving understanding of Australia's obligations under international law, particularly in light of Australia's ratification of the United Nations Convention on the Prevention and Punishment of the Crime of Genocide in 1949 and the increasing international focus on human rights following the Second World War.

The legislative amendment in 1962 allowed Indigenous Australians to enrol to vote in federal elections, a right that was made compulsory for all enrolled voters in Australia in 1924, though it was not compulsory for Indigenous Australians to enrol. However, this change did not instantly translate into widespread political participation among Indigenous communities. Many barriers remained, including widespread discrimination, lack of access to voting facilities in remote areas, and a deep-seated mistrust of government institutions that had, for generations, enacted policies of displacement, assimilation, and separation.

Despite these challenges, the enfranchisement of Indigenous

Australians in 1962 stands as a watershed moment in the nation's journey towards reconciliation and equality. It laid the groundwork for subsequent reforms, including the 1967 referendum which saw an overwhelming majority of Australians vote to amend the constitution to allow the federal government to make laws for Indigenous Australians and to include them in the national census.

The extension of voting rights in 1962 was not just about allowing Indigenous Australians to participate in the democratic process; it was an acknowledgment of their status as citizens and an overdue recognition of their rights. It represented a step towards dismantling the legal and social structures that had long marginalised Indigenous communities and was a critical moment in the ongoing struggle for justice, recognition, and equality for Indigenous Australians.

In reflecting on this chapter of Australian history, it is evident that the 1962 amendment was both a culmination of past activism and a catalyst for future change. It highlighted the enduring strength and resilience of Indigenous Australians in advocating for their rights and set the stage for further advancements in the recognition and protection of these rights. The enfranchisement of Indigenous Australians in federal elections was a significant milestone in the nation's democratic evolution, marking a move towards a more inclusive and equitable society.

The year 1975 remains etched in the annals of Australian political history as the year of the most profound constitutional crisis the nation has ever witnessed. This was the year when Prime Minister Gough Whitlam, leading the Labor government, was dismissed from office by the Governor-General, Sir John Kerr, an event that shook the very foundations of Australia's democracy and left an indelible mark on its political landscape.

Gough Whitlam's government, elected in 1972, had embarked on an ambitious program of reform that sought to radically transform Australian society. The Whitlam government introduced a wide range of policies aimed at social equity, including the establishment of universal healthcare (Medibank), the abolition of university tuition fees, and the introduction of legal aid services. It also made significant strides in foreign policy, notably by withdrawing Australian troops from Vietnam and recognising the People's Republic of China.

However, Whitlam's reformist agenda soon encountered fierce opposition. The Senate, controlled by the opposition Liberal-Country Party coalition, became a battleground for political disputes. By 1975, this opposition had escalated to a point where the Senate refused to pass the supply bills necessary for funding the government, leading to a constitutional impasse. Without these funds, the government would soon be unable to function, unable to pay public servants, or to maintain public services.

The crisis reached its climax on 11th November 1975. In a move that was unprecedented, Governor-General Sir John Kerr exercised his reserve powers under the Australian Constitution to dismiss Prime Minister Gough Whitlam. Kerr appointed the Leader of the Opposition, Malcolm Fraser, as caretaker Prime Minister, conditional upon his ability to secure supply and call a double dissolution election. This decision was made without prior warning to Whitlam and has been a subject of intense debate and analysis ever since.

The dismissal sparked a constitutional and political storm across Australia. Supporters of Whitlam's government were outraged, viewing the Governor-General's actions as a betrayal of democracy and an overreach of his constitutional role. Mass protests and demonstrations ensued, with the steps of Parliament House in Canberra becoming the focal point for public anger and dismay. The phrase "Well may we say 'God save the Queen', because nothing will save the Governor-General" from Whitlam's impromptu speech on the steps of Parliament House, immediately after his dismissal, captured the sentiment of many Australians.

The subsequent election held in December 1975 saw a resounding victory for Malcolm Fraser's Liberal-Country Party coalition, which was interpreted by some as a public endorsement of Kerr's decision. However, the dismissal continued to reverberate through Australian politics and society. It prompted a reevaluation of the role of the Governor-General, the powers of the Senate, and the conventions governing the relationship between these institutions and the elected government.

The dismissal of the Whitlam government remains a controversial chapter in Australian history. It exposed the vulnerabilities in the country's constitutional framework and sparked a debate on the need for reform. Questions about the balance of power between the Commonwealth's executive and its legislature, the role of the Crown in Australia's political system, and the nature of parliamentary democracy itself were brought to the forefront.

In the years that followed, the dismissal influenced discussions on Australia's constitutional future, including debates on becoming a republic and the role of a head of state. It also left a legacy of political activism and engagement among Australians, with an increased awareness of the importance of safeguarding democratic principles and processes.

The events of 1975 underscored the complexities and nuances of Australia's constitutional and political system. The dismissal of Prime Minister Gough Whitlam by Governor-General Sir John Kerr remains a defining moment, a reminder of the tensions that can arise within a parliamentary democracy, and a testament to the enduring nature of political debate and reform in Australia.

In the annals of sporting history, few moments have captured the imagination of a nation and the attention of the world quite like Australia's victory in the 1983 America's Cup. This triumph not only shattered the New York Yacht Club's 132-year stronghold on the coveted trophy but also marked a watershed moment in the history of competitive sailing. The event transcended the realm of sport, symbolising innovation, national pride, and the breaking of long-standing barriers.

The America's Cup, the oldest trophy in international sport, had been dominated by the United States since the inaugural race off the coast of England in 1851. For over a century, challengers from around the globe attempted to wrest the trophy from the grasp of the New York Yacht Club, only to be met with defeat. The competition, therefore, had evolved into a symbol of maritime supremacy and technological prowess.

The Australian challenge was mounted by the Royal Perth Yacht Club, with businessman Alan Bond at the helm of the syndicate for the fourth consecutive challenge. The yacht selected for the task was the innovative Australia II, designed by Ben Lexcen. What set Australia II apart was its revolutionary winged keel, a design so radical and effective that it sparked controversy and debate within the yachting community. This keel provided Australia II with superior speed and manoeuvrability, particularly in the heavy winds and choppy waters characteristic of the racecourse off Newport, Rhode Island.

The 1983 America's Cup was contested in a best-of-seven race format. The defender, Liberty, skippered by Dennis Conner, was a formidable opponent, representing the pinnacle of American yachting and the weight of its winning legacy. The initial races of the series saw intense competition, with both yachts showcasing their speed, design, and the skill of their crews. Australia II, however, faced an uphill battle, trailing Liberty in the early stages of the series.

The resilience and determination of the Australian team, led by skipper John Bertrand, were put to the test. In what became a dramatic and nail-biting series, Australia II mounted a remarkable comeback from a 3-1 deficit, showcasing not only the yacht's technological edge but also the crew's sailing prowess and strategic acumen.

The decisive seventh race, held on 26th September 1983, was a spectacle of competitive sailing at its finest. Australia II and Liberty jostled for position in a tense and closely fought contest, with the lead changing hands multiple times. In the end, it was Australia II that crossed the finish line first, securing a historic victory and ending the longest winning streak in sporting history.

The victory of Australia II was celebrated not just by the team and the Royal Perth Yacht Club but by the entire nation of Australia. It was a moment of immense national pride, uniting Australians in celebration and marking the country's arrival on the world stage in a domain long dominated by the United States. The win was heralded as a triumph of innovation, with the winged keel of Australia II becoming a symbol of Australian ingenuity and a testament to the spirit of challenging the status quo.

The 1983 America's Cup victory had far-reaching implications beyond the immediate euphoria of the win. It transformed the America's Cup from a competition dominated by a single club into a truly international contest, attracting challengers and defenders from across the globe. The event spurred advancements in yacht design and technology, as teams sought to emulate and surpass the innovations that had propelled Australia II to victory.

Moreover, the win inspired a generation of Australians, fostering a deep sense of national pride and a belief in the possibility of achieving greatness on the world stage. It demonstrated the value of teamwork, perseverance, and the relentless pursuit of excellence—qualities that transcended the sport of sailing and resonated with people in all walks of life.

In the annals of Australian sport, the 1983 America's Cup victory stands as a defining moment, a point in time when Australia challenged the might of the New York Yacht Club and emerged victorious, forever altering the course of competitive sailing. The story of Australia II and its crew is a testament to the power of innovation, the spirit of competition, and the enduring allure of the America's Cup.

The 1992 Mabo decision by the High Court of Australia represents one of the most significant legal milestones in the country's history, fundamentally altering the legal landscape regarding land rights and marking a turning point in the recognition of Indigenous Australians' rights. This landmark ruling not only challenged the existing legal framework but also paved the way for a profound reevaluation of the historical narrative surrounding the colonization of Australia and the treatment of its Indigenous peoples.

The case was brought to the High Court by Eddie Koiki Mabo and four other Torres Strait Islanders from Mer (Murray Island) in the Torres Strait. The plaintiffs sought to challenge the legal doctrine of terra nullius, which had declared Australia as land belonging to no one at the time of

British colonization, thereby ignoring the existing rights and occupancy of Indigenous Australians. The case argued for the recognition of native title, the traditional rights to their land that Indigenous Australians had maintained for thousands of years before British settlement.

On 3 June 1992, after a decade of legal proceedings, the High Court delivered its verdict in Mabo v Queensland (No 2). The Court, in a 6 to 1 decision, recognised the existence of native title rights, overturning the terra nullius doctrine and acknowledging that Indigenous rights to land had survived the assertion of sovereignty and the acquisition of land under British colonial rule. The Court found that the Meriam people were entitled to possess, occupy, and use the island of Mer according to their own laws and customs.

The Mabo decision was groundbreaking for several reasons. Legally, it acknowledged the pre-colonial rights and interests of Indigenous Australians to their land, fundamentally challenging the notion that Australian land had been lawfully acquired under the principles of British settlement. It highlighted the necessity for Australian law to accommodate the pre-existing socio-legal systems of Indigenous peoples, recognising their unique connection to the land.

Socially and politically, the Mabo decision had a profound impact on Australian society, sparking a nationwide debate on Indigenous rights, land justice, and reconciliation. It forced the Australian public and its leaders to confront the historical injustices inflicted upon Indigenous communities and opened up discussions on how to redress these wrongs. The ruling was met with mixed reactions; while it was celebrated by Indigenous communities and their supporters as a long-overdue recognition of their rights, it also prompted concern and opposition among some sectors, particularly regarding the implications for land ownership and use.

In response to the Mabo decision, the Australian Government, led by Prime Minister Paul Keating, enacted the Native Title Act 1993. This legislation aimed to implement the High Court's decision, providing a framework for recognising and protecting native title across Australia. The Act established the National Native Title Tribunal, a mechanism through which Indigenous

Australians could make claims of native title over lands and waters.

The legacy of the Mabo decision extends far beyond its legal implications. It has been instrumental in fostering a greater understanding and respect for Indigenous cultures and histories within the broader Australian community. It has also inspired further legal and political activism surrounding Indigenous rights, including subsequent landmark cases and the ongoing movement for treaty and sovereignty rights.

The Mabo decision's significance is commemorated annually on 3 June, Mabo Day, as part of National Reconciliation Week in Australia. It serves as a reminder of Eddie Mabo's tireless fight for justice and the enduring importance of recognising the rights and dignity of Indigenous Australians. The ruling stands as a testament to the possibility of change and the power of law as a tool for rectifying historical injustices, symbolising a step towards reconciliation and the recognition of the oldest continuous cultures on earth.

The Port Arthur massacre of 1996 is a somber and pivotal chapter in Australian history, marking a watershed moment in the nation's approach to gun control and public safety. On 28th April 1996, in the tranquil setting of the historic Port Arthur site in Tasmania, a lone gunman opened fire, resulting in the tragic loss of 35 lives and leaving 23 others wounded. This devastating event shocked the Australian public and galvanized the government into implementing one of the world's most comprehensive and effective gun control measures in history.

Prior to this tragic day, Australia's gun laws were considered relatively lenient, with the regulations around firearm ownership varying significantly between states and territories. The ease with which individuals could acquire firearms, including high-powered semi-automatic rifles, was a growing concern. However, it took the magnitude of the Port Arthur tragedy to bring about national consensus on the need for stringent gun control.

In the aftermath of the massacre, newly elected Prime Minister John Howard, leading a conservative coalition government, took decisive action to overhaul the country's gun laws. Recognising the need for a unified approach to prevent such a tragedy from occurring again, the government proposed the National Firearms Agreement (NFA) in May 1996, just weeks after the massacre. The NFA sought to introduce strict gun control measures across all Australian states and territories, marking a significant shift in the nation's attitude towards firearm ownership.

Key provisions of the NFA included a ban on the importation, possession, sale, and use of all automatic and semi-automatic firearms, except under certain controlled conditions. It also established a comprehensive system for firearm licensing and registration, requiring all firearm owners to demonstrate a genuine reason for owning a weapon, which did not include self-defence. Additionally, the NFA implemented a nationwide buyback scheme, funded by a one-off levy on federal taxes, which resulted in the surrender and destruction of over 600,000 firearms.

The implementation of the NFA was met with widespread public support, as well as opposition from some quarters, particularly among gun owners and shooting enthusiasts. However, the Australian government's firm stance, coupled with widespread media coverage and public discourse on the need to prevent future tragedies, ensured the successful enactment and enforcement of the new laws.

The impact of the NFA and the accompanying gun law reforms has been profound and lasting. Studies and analyses conducted in the years following the reform have shown a significant reduction in gun-related deaths in Australia, including homicides and suicides. Additionally, there has been no mass shooting in Australia since the implementation of the NFA, a testament to the effectiveness of the measures introduced.

The Port Arthur massacre and the subsequent gun law reforms represent a critical juncture in Australia's social and political history. The swift and decisive action taken by the government and supported by the Australian public demonstrates the capacity for significant policy change in the face of tragedy. The legacy of the reforms extends beyond the reduction in gun violence; it stands as a powerful example of national unity and the collective will to protect the safety and wellbeing of the community.

This chapter in Australian history underscores the importance of responsive and responsible governance, the value of public safety over individual interests, and the enduring impact of collective action in the face of adversity. The legacy of Port Arthur and the reforms it inspired continue to resonate, serving as a reminder of the lives lost and the importance of vigilance in upholding the principles of peace and security in society.

In the year 2000, Sydney, Australia's largest and most vibrant city, was thrust into the global spotlight as the host of the Summer Olympic Games. This monumental event, held from the 15th of September to the 1st of October, was celebrated as the "Millennium Games" and marked a defining moment in Australia's cultural and sporting history. The successful bid and subsequent hosting of the Games underscored Australia's standing on the world stage, showcasing its capabilities in organising a global event of immense scale and complexity while highlighting the nation's spirit, diversity, and natural beauty.

The selection of Sydney by the International Olympic Committee (IOC) in 1993 over other candidate cities was a testament to Australia's thorough and compelling bid, which promised not only to deliver exceptional Games but also to leave a lasting legacy for the city and the wider community. The Sydney Games were the second Olympics held in Australia, following the Melbourne Games of 1956, and they reflected the country's deep love for sport and its commitment to the Olympic ideals of excellence, friendship, and respect.

Preparations for the Games were extensive, involving massive infrastructure projects and urban renewal initiatives that transformed Sydney. The heart of the Games was the Sydney Olympic Park at Homebush Bay, a former industrial wasteland that was redeveloped into a state-of-the-art sporting complex. Facilities such as the Olympic Stadium, Aquatic Centre, and

Velodrome set new standards for Olympic venues, combining innovative design with environmental sustainability.

The Sydney Olympics attracted more than 10,000 athletes from 199 nations, making it the largest Olympic Games ever held at the time. The competition was fierce and showcased outstanding performances across a wide range of sports. Memorable moments included the Australian women's water polo team clinching gold in the sport's Olympic debut, Cathy Freeman winning the 400 metres in front of a jubilant home crowd, and the US team's dramatic victory in the men's 4x100 metres freestyle relay, breaking the world record.

The Games were also notable for their spirit of inclusiveness and harmony.

The Paralympics, held in October following the Olympics, received unprecedented attention and support, further emphasising the event's legacy of promoting diversity and equality in sport. Additionally, the Sydney Games were marked by a significant effort to celebrate Australia's Indigenous cultures, with the opening ceremony featuring a spectacular and moving tribute to the country's Aboriginal and Torres Strait Islander peoples.

Sydney 2000 set a new benchmark for environmental responsibility in mega-event planning. Initiatives such as the use of solar power, water conservation measures, and extensive public transport options were integral to the Games' operations, reflecting a commitment to sustainability that would influence future Olympic hosts.

The Games were widely regarded as a triumph, with IOC President Juan Antonio Samaranch declaring them the "best Olympic Games ever" during the closing ceremony. The success of the Sydney Olympics was attributed not only to the flawless execution of the event and the athletes' exceptional performances but also to the enthusiastic participation of the Australian people. Volunteers, dubbed the "Games Force," provided warm hospitality to visitors and athletes alike, embodying the friendly and open spirit for which Australians are known.

The legacy of the Sydney 2000 Olympics extends beyond the tangible improvements to the city's infrastructure. The Games fostered a sense of national pride and unity, showcasing Australia's cultural diversity and its capacity for innovation and excellence. They left an indelible mark on Sydney and its people, creating memories that continue to inspire and resonate two decades later. The Sydney Olympics epitomised the transformative power of sport, serving as a reminder of its ability to bring people together, transcend differences, and celebrate the human spirit.

The tapestry of Australian history, woven from the threads of pivotal events spanning over two centuries, illustrates a nation's journey through moments of challenge, transformation, and triumph. From the ancient stewardship of its lands by Indigenous Australians to the modern era marked by significant social, political, and cultural milestones, Australia's story is one of resilience, innovation, and progress.

The recognition of Indigenous land rights in the landmark Mabo decision, the nationwide reforms following the Port Arthur massacre, and the unifying spirit of the Sydney Olympics are but a few chapters in this rich narrative. Each event, in its own way, has contributed to shaping the nation's identity, values, and place on the world stage.

The evolution of Australia from a collection of British colonies to a federation marked by the struggle for democratic rights, the recognition of Indigenous Australians, and the development of a distinctive national character reflects a broader journey towards justice, equality, and inclusion. The challenges faced and the victories achieved highlight the dynamic and evolving nature of Australian society.

The stories of Australia are not without their complexities and controversies. The path has been marked by moments of conflict, introspection, and debate, driving a continuous effort to reconcile with the past and build a more equitable and inclusive future. The resilience of the Indigenous peoples, the courage of those who have stood up for civil liberties, and the collective spirit of a nation willing to confront its shortcomings and embrace change are enduring qualities that define the Australian experience.

As Australia continues to navigate the challenges of the 21st century, the lessons of history remain a guiding light. The nation's journey, characterised by the pursuit of progress within a framework of respect for the environment, diversity, and human rights, offers valuable insights into the power of community, the importance of sustainability, and the unending quest for a fair and just society.

In conclusion, the fabric of Australian history is rich and diverse, marked by moments of profound significance that continue to influence the nation's course. It is a history that invites reflection, encourages resilience, and inspires a continued commitment to shaping a future that honours the past while boldly embracing the possibilities of tomorrow. Through the collective efforts of its people, Australia stands as a testament to the enduring spirit of humanity's capacity for growth, adaptation, and the ceaseless pursuit of a better world.

Milton Keynes UK
Ingram Content Group UK Ltd.
UKHW050701270324
440147UK00006B/165